Praise for *Toxemia*

"*Toxemia* is astonishing. It's difficult to use positive adjectives for something so searing and widespread as toxicity in all its forms as it is portrayed in this book. But what can be said is that we need this book. We need 'a pattern that is only legible' to McNair. If nothing else, in this undetermined narrative, we may read our multiple selves, our own fragilities to systemic damage and unutterable forces beyond our control."

— Madhur Anand, Governor General's Literary Award–winning author of *This Red Line Goes Straight to Your Heart*

"*Toxemia* is simultaneously a history in/of medicine, a feminist rallying cry, and a raw but scalpel-sharp work of poetry. A genre-blurring text that boldly bloodies lines between poetic and reproductive bodies, between archive and lyric, between manifesto and song, between autoethnography and free verse. A bodypoem flex."

— Sarah de Leeuw, author of *Lot*

"How much pressure can build in language before the story of women's health blows apart? In *Toxemia*, Christine McNair tests the narrative as if it were a problem patient. She charts the events that bring her close to death several times with the skill of the most intuitive midwives and rigorous clinicians, though representation is not diagnostic. This is a beautiful etiological study."

— Elee Kraljii Gardiner, author of *Trauma Head* and *Against Death: 35 Essays on Living*

Praise for *Charm*
Winner of the Archibald Lampman Award

"In *Charm*, McNair shows us unique truths in unexpected and mesmerizing ways, compelling our attention again and again."
— Archibald Lampman Award jury citation

"These poems hover around an overarching theme of making and unmaking, but their expansiveness allows for each to remain distinct and precise."
— *Canadian Literature*

"*Charm* is a skillfully crafted collection and will surely captivate any lover of language."
— *Vallum*

Praise for *Conflict*
Finalist for the City of Ottawa Book Award
Finalist for the Archibald Lampman Award

"McNair has got a near ear. Her textural play is fantastic... This is a terrifically loaded book."
— *Arc Poetry*

"*Conflict* is a book that risks much, personally and otherwise, between methodical approach and an eye on pulling apart meaning, style and syntax. The poems are physical, forcing a comprehension of the self and the world, and the relationships between."
— *Prairie Fire*

TOXEMIA

Christine McNair

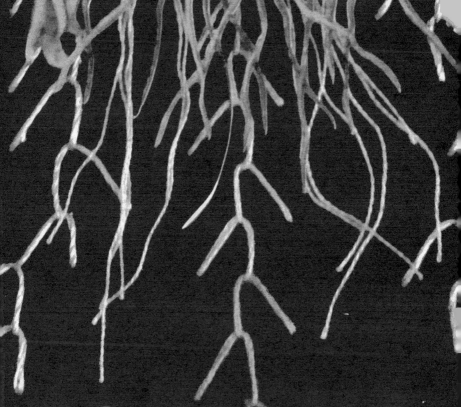

TOXEMIA

Christine McNair

Book*hug Press | Toronto 2024

Library and Archives Canada Cataloguing in Publication

Title: Toxemia / Christine McNair.

Names: McNair, Christine, 1978– author.

Identifiers: Canadiana (print) 20240345673
Canadiana (ebook) 2024034569X
    ISBN 9781771669146 (softcover)
    ISBN 9781771669214 (EPUB)
Subjects: LCGFT: Autobiographical poetry. | LCGFT: Poetry.
Classification: LCC PS8625.N33 T69 2024 | DDC C811/.6—dc23

The production of this book was made possible through the
generous assistance of the Canada Council for the Arts and the
Ontario Arts Council. Book*hug Press also acknowledges the
support of the Government of Canada through the Canada Book
Fund and the Government of Ontario through the Ontario Book
Publishing Tax Credit and the Ontario Book Fund.

Book*hug Press acknowledges that the land on which we operate is
the traditional territory of many nations, including the Mississaugas
of the Credit, the Anishnabeg, the Chippewa, the Haudenosaunee,
and the Wendat peoples. We recognize the enduring presence
of many diverse First Nations, Inuit, and Métis peoples, and are
grateful for the opportunity to meet and work on this territory.

Book*hug Press

For Lady Sybil

In einer früheren Veröffentlichung habe ich die Eklampsie nicht
ohne Anflug von Ironie eine Krankheit der Theorien gennant.
In an earlier publication I called eclampsia, not without a touch of
irony, a disease of theories.

> —Paul Zweifel in *Handbuch der Geburtshilfe*, Volume 2,
> Albert Döderlein, Karl Baisch, Verlag von J. F. Bergmann, 1916

There is something so touching in the death of a woman who has
recently given birth to her child... It is a sort of desecration for an
accouche to die.

> —Charles Meigs (1848) in *Death in Childbirth: An International*
> *Study of Maternal Care and Maternal Mortality (1800–1950),*
> Irvine Loudon, Clarendon Press, 1992

contents

invocation 11

symptoms

imparfait 15

déjà vécu 17

presque vu 19

jamais vu 21

déjà vu 25

déjà vu 29

déjà rêvé 33

imperatif 35

déjà entendu 37

overlap 40

présent 43

presentation

timbre 47

futur proche 51

collateral information 55

conditionnel 61

marantic 63

endo 65

carditis 67

foliate 71

risk factors

subjonctif 77

egg clairomancy 79

it's nothing like fire 87

scry 89

ex communication 93

nesting dolls 95

plus-que-parfait 107

clever clogs 109

zlata baba 117

passé composé 119

pacem 121

treatment

get up 127

look 129

loop 131

records 133

passé simple 135

intercession
intermission 137

tin soldiers 141

treatment table 143

futur simple 145

primigravida 147

multiparous 149

nesting doll 155

consequence 159

Endnotes 163

List of Figures 165

Glossary of Terms 169

Acknowledgements 173

About the Author 175

Plaudit in teris. domus omipotetis olimpi.
Na; noua pycies celo diuiditur alto.
Xps te rogat. ut uideas lucem istius seculi.
In nomie. patris. ɇ filij. ɇ sps sci amen.
Exi infans. xps te uocat. In nomine filij exi
infans. xps te ducit. in nomine sps sancti
exi infans. xps te regit. et ad batisma inui
tat. qui pro te passus est. et de latere suo aq
uam batismi produxit. et baptismum suo
sanguine rubricauit. Elisabeth peperit io
hanem. Anna peperit mariam. Maria uirgo
peperit xpm. saluatorem mundi. qui te lib
eret. N. a partu et doloribus. tuis. amen.
Si es masculus. ul femina. uiuus. ul mortu
us. ueni foras. quia xps te uocat. In noie.
patris. et filij. et sps sci. amen. Pater. est.
alpha. et. O. filius. est uita. Spiritussc̃s
est medicina :. Deo gra   et   as.

Sancta Margareta sic orante et dicente, draco apperuit os suum super caput beate Margarite et lingua eius pertingens usque ad calcaneum beate Margarete et deglutivit eam. Sed facto signo crucis draco ille terribilis permedium est divisus et ipsa exivit de utero eius illesa sine dolore aliquo. St Margaret praying and chanting in this manner, the dragon opened its mouth above the saint's head and stretching out its tongue as far as St Margaret's heel it swallowed her. But once the sign of the cross had been made that fearful dragon split open in the middle and she came forth (*exivit*) from its womb unharmed and without any pain. Sancta Margareta sic orante et dicente, draco apperuit os suum super caput beate Margarite et lingua eius pertingens usque ad calcaneum beate Margarete et deglutivit eam. Sed facto signo crucis draco ille terribilis permedium est divisus et ipsa exivit de utero eius illesa sine dolore aliquo. St Margaret praying and chanting in this manner, the dragon opened its mouth above the saint's head and stretching out its tongue as far as St Margaret's heel it swallowed her. But once the sign of the cross had been made that fearful dragon split open in the middle and she came forth (*exivit*) from its womb unharmed and without any pain. Sancta Margareta sic orante et dicente, draco ∞

Exi infans. Come forth infant.[1]

symptoms

imparfait

*The imparfait (continuous past) emphasizes the progression
or the regular repetition of an action in the past.*

I sit in the dark and I wait. I sit in the dark and the children are
sleeping. Two-year-old curled up shell-shaped on my hip. Newborn
in her side-carred crib, sleep-twitchy and precious. I've called my
mother. It's 4 a.m. I wait in the dark because I worry I'm dying. I
don't wake my husband yet, will do so closer to my mother's arrival.
I don't want to die between my children. The bps are up and my
feet twitch. My brain lit up and hard electric, the same as before.
The pain in the side. The brain lit up and electric and a pressing
sense of doom and headache in the bones that goes on and on and
won't stop. The numbers on the clock double themselves up and
dance around. The brain is lit up and my legs twitch, and the aura
I remember from before from so long before, from the seizures as
a kid, and the seizures when I was bulimic, and the seizure after
playing the fainting game. The sense of cliff. Brain is all lit up with
pain and I worry I'm dying and I don't want to seize between my
children and there's nothing but waiting in the dark and it all takes
too long and I'm waiting.

I sit in the dark and I wait. I sit in the dark and the children are sleeping. Five-year-old curled up shell-shaped on my hip. Three-year-old in her side-carred crib, sleep-twitchy and precious. I've not called anyone. It's 1 a.m. I wait in the dark because I worry I'm dying. My husband isn't here, he's taking care of my father-in-law at the farm. I don't want to die between my children. The bps are up and my face tingles. A pressing sense of doom that goes on and on and won't stop. The numbers on the clock double themselves up and dance around. The brain is dark. The sense of cliff. Brain processes weakness and tingling and I worry I'm dying and I don't want to die between my children and there's nothing but waiting in the dark and it all takes too long and I'm waiting. I turn on my side and turn on a meditation app. Pour lavender oil on my throat.

déjà vécu

"The main features of the Stroganoff regime were very heavy sedation combined with magnesium sulphate and the isolation of the patient in a darkened and totally quiet room where she was attended by staff tiptoeing in stocking feet and peering in the dark. It was based on the theory that stimuli, auditory and visual, were the triggers for eclampsia. The method gained credence because it was so dramatic. The patient was treated as if she was an unexploded bomb. Cynics said the advantage of the regime was that the staff were unable to see in the dark just how bad the patient's condition really was. It was a method used extensively until the 1950s."[2]

Lone dark, magnesium sulfate stems the tide. Keeps nerve flicks at bay. The nurse is at the station, she sits watching me all night in the dark. The baby is not here. The baby is not here. The baby is at home. My milk comes in. Hurts. They have to help me use the pump. Head breaks. I can hear babies wailing from the ceiling in the middle of the night and am disoriented. Soft cries and half cries. Where's my baby? The baby's not here, remember? The

17

baby's at home. The nurse shakes me out of a gasp, asks if I'm okay, critical thinning of her eyes. Bad dream. It's only after my second birth, when I'm readmitted into that same room for postpartum preeclampsia that I notice the vent in the ceiling. All the sounds of the ward, the labouring women, the babies, and their machines, titrate down over the bed. I get into bed. I grip the rails.

presque vu

I clench my teeth. I breathe in past panic. I must maintain a good face. I must be reasonable. The doctor must find me clear. I must research enough to ask good questions but not too many.

At least there are visible growths on my heart. Nodules. Clots. Vegetations. Depends which doctor you ask as to preferred terminology. Non-bacterial endocarditis means no fever, means an underlying reason. Lupus. Metastasized cancer. Blood-clotting issue. Thrombophilia. My body loves clots.

Thrombo, the clotting of blood. Philia, love. My body loves clots. I am thrombophilic. We hope I am thrombophilic and the blood thinners will fix it. I heart clots.

Read: *prognosis poor, due to the underlying cause.* Read: *rare, typically found post-mortem.*

They test me more than once for lupus, and more than once I come back negative, they test again and will test again. The thrombosis doctor is laissez-faire. Too breezy. I try not to show my irritation. Nothing is truly explained. There will be more tests.

Heparin builds a yellow moon on my belly. I dream of wheat.

jamais vu

Lady Sybil's ankles are swollen and she seems muddled. *It's all just as it should be.*

Lady Sybil is in distress. *They're fine.*

Do you not find the baby small? *Not unusually so.*

And the ankles? *Maybe she has thick ankles. Lots of women do.*

But she does not.

Am I on duty, Dr. Clarkson?

What?

Only I swear I'm not on duty, otherwise I wouldn't be lying here. (SYBIL HYPERVENTILATES)

She can't hear me. *This is eclampsia.* Please breathe love. She can't breathe. No no no no no. Do something. Help her. *There's nothing to be done.* Do something. Help her. *Once the seizures have started there's nothing to be done.*

Please no. No no no no no no. Please luv. Please wake up love. Please don't leave me. No no no no no no. This cannot be.

In a study, volunteers were asked to write the word *door* 30 times in 60 seconds. Sixty-eight per cent of the subjects began to doubt that *door* was a real word.

But you see no complications here? *None at all. Lady Sybil is a perfect model of health and beauty.*

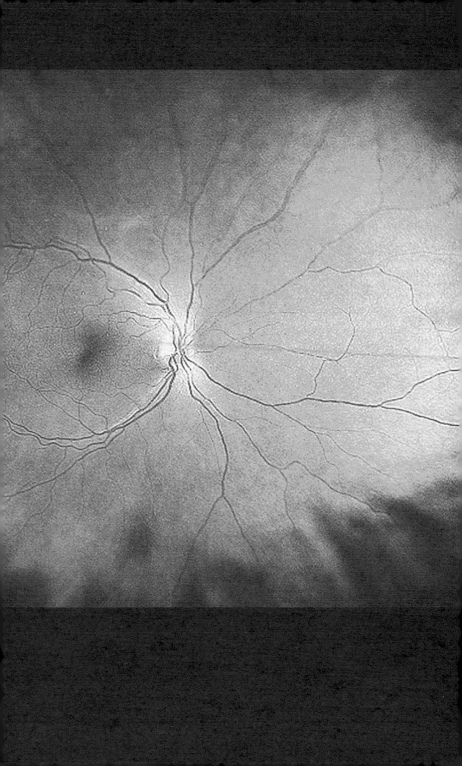

déjà vu

Mama, wake up! It's Sybil. **(HYPERVENTILATING) (TRIES TO SPEAK)** Can you hear me, darling? It's Tom. **I should be getting up.** Darling, all you need to do is rest. **(SHE CRIES OUT)** Sybil? **My head...! My head!** Sybil? Let me bathe your forehead. **It hurts!** What's happening? Oh, God. Oh, God! God, no, no! What the hell is happening? Sybil? She can't hear me. Sybil? Sybil, it's Mary. Can you hear me? It looks as if—It looks as if what? This is eclampsia. Sybil? It cannot be, Sir Philip. You were so sure. She can't hear me. This is unbelievable. Darling... Somebody do something! The human life is unpredictable. But you were so sure! What can we do? Help her, help her, please! **(SYBIL HYPERVENTILATES)** Oh, God, no! Dr. Clarkson, shall we take her to the hospital? There's nothing that can be done. It's not possible, not these days! Once the seizures have started, there's nothing to be done. You don't agree, do you? Please don't leave me! Help her! Help her, please! She can't breathe. Please, just breathe. There has to be something worth trying! Please! Come on, come on. Breathe, love. Come on. Sybil? Listen, it's me, my darling. All you need to do is breathe. We've given her morphine, and atropine. What's happening? Please breathe, love! Please! She can't breathe. Oh, no, no! Please! Oh, no! Please, love. No, no! Please wake up.

Please don't leave me. Please wake up, love. Please don't leave me!
Please don't leave me, love! No! Oh, God! Please, love. But this can't
be. She's 24 years old. This cannot be.

(BABY CRIES)

I can't stop thinking about Lady Sybil.

déjà vu

"Blood-letting remained a staple in the prevention and treatment of preeclampsia-eclampsia during the early 1800s. The amount and frequency of blood-letting depended on the strength of the patient and symptom severity. Bleeding from the arm was attempted initially, but if convulsions continued, bleeding was repeated. In some cases the jugular vein or temporal artery were opened in an attempt to stop convulsions."[3]

Between pregnancies, I went for an assessment because I was unwell, and I suspected it was postpartum depression.

I have a significant history of depression.

They always want the ticker tape past history: DSM BDI MDD PSY MSW MDD ED IRF SIB IOP MDD BDD ED CBT MDD IOP CBT PSY MDD IOP PSY PTSD IOP MBCT ST. I hate telling it. I can see in their faces how long it is. I can see in their faces the hard math. This particular psychologist stops listening once I mention the history of self-harm.

She does not refer me to help for my postpartum depression. She suggests I seek out psychological therapy aimed at people with borderline personality disorder. She does not refer to my lack of sleep (two to four hours per night), the hormones, my uncontrolled endocrine disorder, which can cause depression, the lactation problems, or my PTSD after the difficult postpartum preeclampsia. She does not recommend perinatal mental health support services. She is unaware of peer groups for postpartum mental health. She does not acknowledge that self-harm can occur for reasons other than borderline personality disorder. She does not look me in the eye.

She stands me up on the second consult. She forgets my appointment. I wait in the empty waiting room with no music. I need to nurse. I leaf through *Chatelaine*s. I tiptoe to the reception to an open window to ask where why where. I call to say I won't ever be coming back. I go to my family doctor and ask to be put back on my antidepressants. Even though they're a class C drug (unknown unknown unknown) and I'm still nursing. She weighs the risks/benefits. Agrees.

I improve markedly after just a few weeks back on my medication. I do not self-harm. The baby is fine even though she drinks my milk.

I am now more afraid of telling doctors my history.

déjà rêvé

"Many female ailments were attributed to the wandering womb. Hippocrates believed that a dried up uterus wandered the body in search of moisture, Plato viewed the uterus as an animal that wandered because it was sexually unsatisfied and desired to make children. Regardless of reason, as the uterus wandered the body, it was capable of wreaking havoc upon the liver, stomach, spleen, lungs, and head, ultimately leading to disease."[4]

Don't stop the bells. The bells keep. They clang out the things we won't say, the endless. They clang but then stop or we wouldn't have heard them. And the sisters in wait, they lie up against the bones of the church. Their hungry wandering wombs restless perhaps in their elbow or deep-seated wrists.

They cannot examine themselves properly. Wise women round the gate.

Ring loud the bells. Don't stop. It's time. It's just time.

imperatif

We use this form for demands and orders, when addressing one or more people directly.

I hate being pregnant. Do not get pregnant.

Constant nausea plus thick swell, the belly burns the bones. Sciatica. Back pain, nausea, heart burn, insomnia, carpal tunnel symptoms. Vomit at work in my garbage bin, in my cubicle. Vomit in the back hallway bathroom. Vomit in every bathroom. There is no escape from the vomit. Ever.

déjà entendu

Sudden flash—eclampsia of lightning. Nearly all the deities of lightning are men. Almost none are female.

The Madonna and baby lighthouses on the hill. We drive out and my chest is pressured and I worry the distance to the small hospital in Humboldt. Why did I get in the car when I didn't feel well?

I wanted to see the mother protected.

The sky streaked with contrails. The blue of it and the flat sedge on the hill. The stones embedded, that we try to embed with meaning. Lightning rods embedded in the hill to safeguard the mother and child from lightning strikes. She had already been hit twice. There was a bench for the pilgrims.

Someone climbed up to steal the bench. Someone climbed up to cut short the lightning rods to take the copper. The remnants are rough-hewn in the hill, like hollow copper moons. Stones between. They feel rough when I touch them.

The mother and child are exposed. They Latinate out salvos of compassion to the sick on the side of the plinth.

I leave a dime on the hill. The hollow moons upset me.

The hill itself was important to the local Indigenous community, but the whys of it are not recorded by the monks. Or deliberately misremembered. It's why the Madonna sits here. The Father thinks it might have involved a girl who was buried in the hill.

We overlook the fields. The stones in the hill speak. We can't hear them properly.

overlap

heart attack	depression	third trimester
Pain or discomfort that spreads to the shoulder, arm, back, neck, jaw, teeth, or sometimes the upper belly	Unexplained physical problems, such as back pain or headaches	Backaches
Fatigue	Tiredness	Fatigue
Heartburn or indigestion		Heartburn
	Sleep disturbances, including insomnia or sleeping too much	Insomnia
Sense of impending doom		
	Anxiety, agitation or restlessness	
Shortness of breath		Shortness of breath
Light-headedness or sudden dizziness	Slowed thinking, speaking, or body movements	
		Headaches
Cold sweat		

preeclampsia	anxiety
Pain in the upper belly, usually under the ribs on the right side	Chest pain
	Feeling weak or tired
Nausea or vomiting	(GI) problems
	Trouble sleeping
Sense of impending doom	Sense of impending danger or doom
Anxiety, agitation, or restlessness	Feeling nervous, restless or tense
Shortness of breath	Breathing rapidly (hyperventilation)
Confusion	Trouble thinking and concentrating
Severe headaches	
	Sweating and trembling

présent

The présent corresponds to the present tense in English. We mostly use this tense to speak about the present and the future.

I watch the ceiling tick out in front of my eyes. The gurney rattles in the hallways and makes a faint warm screech when it turns. The attendants wouldn't let me walk to the ward.

The lights are bright and I'm on a gurney and the ceiling is ticking away in front of me. The baby is at home. She is with her father. My mother, she is here. She is downstairs somewhere on her cellphone, gnashing her fingers while she updates my father. Or is she gone already? Has she left to check on my husband?

Here then there. The same ward where I gave birth only five days before. The same smells, the same faint uncertainty. But no antici-pation, only lights.

To shine forth – last year's almost-end. Or almost-stroke. Or almost-seizure. Possible failures: liver, kidneys. Now – increased risk of cardiovascular death. 2× more likely. Heart worn thin.

Dreaming in a mag sulfate haze of Margaret Kilgallen, who died of cancer days after giving birth to her daughter. Her large-scale letterforms eating up the sky.

Her sly folk ladies with full ladles.

presentation

timbre

When I need to cry, I watch clips from *The Voice*.

I can't cry. I look at clips of people singing to the backs of the chairs. They've turned the chairs around so the judges don't pick purely based on looks. Or won't be swayed by looks.

I only watch the ones where the chairs turn. Where the musicians sway to the songs or look shocked or fall off the chairs.

The singers plead their case to the backs of the chairs. They swing or they don't. They rip their throats out climbing too wide a range or too long a note. They drag open the notes and scrape them over the coals. Their families cluttered in the green room, bouncing or crying when the chairs turn. The lights flash. You see the struggle in the crying, or I create the struggle, the hard work. In the parents especially. You see the child grow up in front of them. You see the little sister's struggle to keep it together.

They shriek. They explode with pride. It is guttural. It feels like a permanent victory.

Singers we'd know or don't or could figure out. Faces that we fake familiarity with. We pretend we know them. We are fond of their quirks. We examine their drinks.

The songs are familiar. The songs are terrible. Or old. Some are repeats, the same songs blipping up, the same same same, the same slow pull of emotion. The possibility, the sick nostalgia, the avoidance. The feelings contained in a snippet. Superficial. Temporary victories and the unpleasantness of hard shift into a few minutes.

One of the international singers is a nun. Her fellow nuns shriek in excitement.

Knowing glances to fellow judges, shifting in their seats, peeking round the corner, rolling their shoulders to the music. I can't always cry when I should. If I cry, I might not stop.

LOW AFFECT LOW AFFECT LOW AFFECT

It's called control.

There's Christina Grimmie though. Her version of "Wrecking Ball" tearing up the stage in a safe way: in a controlled way but cute. She had a big range. Shot in a murder-suicide by an obsessed fan. Died at 22 in Orlando. Still aching for sun. She was opening her arms to give him a hug. She died just before the Pulse shooting and then the child alligator horror at Disney. A horror sinking under other horrors. Grief layered over grief.

Janice Freeman dying of a blood clot at the heart. Lupus. Cervical Cancer. Complication of pneumonia. A pulmonary embolism.

Beverly McClellan from season one dying of endometrial cancer. Singing Janis Joplin's "(Take Another) Little Piece of My Heart" in the blind audition. Fought a "brave battle."

I make myself listen to them sing, over and over, triumphant.

If you go into any subject in depth, you fall into the things you're trying to avoid.

In *The Voice*, what is appealing and also awful is the bodylessness of the voice. The absence of the body, at least until the chairs turn around and the judges begin to watch. In some of the international versions, the judges hide behind a cloak rather than the gimmick of turning chairs. They had to design those chairs. Would it have been too simple to just turn a chair around instead of designing automated ones that swivel? Too awkward? Too much likelihood of damage? Would standing have taken too much out of the judges?

Sometimes I have figure skaters or gymnasts in my head. They ricochet round a rink or a gym, in ways my body was never capable of. They are ecstatic. This often happens when a song I like comes on the radio. More often than not, it's the skater, some residual influence from seeing Elizabeth Manley and her flight of the bumblebee when I was ten, bip-bipping around the Calgary arena. Tight little shots of spins and jumps with athletic thighs. In these invisible moments that do not exist, my body is strong and my mind is clear.

In writing, we talk about finding our voice. Which voice. Whose. And is it disembodied and floating listless back over me? My voice paraded forward out of me in synthetic ribbon—fleshless me-coloured thoughts. What of my voice is left when the body is gone? I don't know.

futur proche

The futur proche is used to talk about actions in the near future.

In the Heart Institute, my machine beeps without cause. It beeps unattached to me. It's just for vitals, and it floats on its own like a cloud. Or rather, hovers over me. Beeping intermittently. It beeps. It insists. It doesn't exist in relation to me. It is calling out like a lamb to its mother. It is its own defective satellite. It sings.

My vitals are for the most part normal. My blood work is normal. My chest pain is not normal. It has been increasing in intensity. It has led to the feeling of a 100-pound weight on my chest. I am not having a heart attack. It is my asthma. It is anxiety. It is indigestion. It is my heart. It is my lungs. It is my brain. It is the fae. It is an excess of mercury. It is a familial curse. It is a small elephant curled onto my breastbone. What is it.

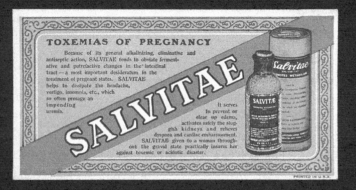

I know there are growths on my heart valve. And they don't make sense. They're odd because they don't match my blood. I don't have lupus. They should be lupus bumps. They could be cancer bumps. I don't have cancer. Rheumatic heart disease? Writ in pencil.

They're culturing my blood. Will there be something there.
They'll be doing a PET. Will there be something there.
They scan my head. Will there be something there.

My questions all have periods instead of question marks. I'm afraid if I ask them, there will be no answers. So they dead stop.

The right side of my face tingles. Do I tell the nurse or will she assume I'm hysterical. I'm not good at telling my symptoms to doctors because I'm afraid they won't believe me. I don't know.

My INR is up to 2.0. That is good. Finally. At a dose of 20 mg of Warfarin.

Please let there be something that can be found and treated. I can't keep experiencing this breathlessness and chest pain without explanation. If it's anxiety, then give me therapy and a pill. I don't care.

It just has to stop. I'm drowning in the unexplained. I would rather be clear. I would rather be certain. I would rather not be this impossible.

My presentation does not make sense. My presentation. My presentation. LOW AFFECT.

I think I'm telling people with my face when I'm not. I think I'm being clear with my symptoms when I'm not. I've chewed off the end of my own telephone wire. What is wrong with the signals.

My face/cheek on the right is tingling. Am I just an anxious weirdo. That would be great.

collateral information

When I was little, there was, in the schoolyard, a small nearly dead tree with a gaping hole in one side. I called it a wishing tree and, depending on the season, I would 'feed' it grass, fallen leaves, or snow, muttering secrets into the bark.

I also ripped down vines that were growing at the back of the schoolyard and wound them into wreaths. Had a couple odd years in elementary school where I didn't want to play with anyone.

I didn't know the English words to the Lord's Prayer or "O Canada" until I was eight or so. I only knew the French version from my immersion school.

At 16, I threw my favourite bra into Lake Ontario on a dare and regretted it instantly.

I still sometimes use my hands when figuring out the 9× multiplications.

The only physical fight I've ever had was with Andrea when we were 10 or 11. She bloodied my nose. We somehow became best friends.

I gained then lost a lot of weight in the past few years, but I can't see the difference. It is never enough. It is none of your business. It doesn't matter. A body is a body is a body is a body.

I had several febrile seizures as a kid, and doctors thought I might be epileptic.

My seizure threshold is lower than most. I made the mistake of playing the fainting game on my grade nine school trip to New York, in a room full of 'enhanced' students playing the fainting game and lighting hairspray on fire. I seized and ended the game.

I had a problem along those lines in 2009, the first since that grade nine episode, due to some medication issues and low electrolytes. All better now.

Sue and I printed a miniature letterpress book. From friends/family, we collected skipping songs (ones they could remember) and printed it on a Vandercook.

I did the MS Read-a-Thon as a kid. My uncle Richard made the mistake of saying he'd pay $5 per volume. By the end, he owed me $600. I let him off the hook.

Once in school we made full-size paper dolls of ourselves. An out-line sketched on butcher's paper, rolled out. How intent I was to make her like me but prettier. The hair was the most difficult part, curls uneven and unravelling back, no definition. I felt sad and dis-satisfied with the final portrait. My parents did not recognize me in the image.

I hated selling Girl Guide cookies.

My bookbinding tutor in London had to buy more bandages for the studio because of me. Bookbinding involves many sharp things. I believe he said he'd never had a student, ever, harm themselves as much as I did. Number one rule of bookbinding: don't bleed on the book.

When I felt sad as a teenager, I would watch the Disney *Alice in Wonderland* film or *Simpsons* episodes I'd taped on VHS off CBC. Earl Grey to wash down Mr. Christie's teething biscuits.

When I was home with wracking period cramps, I'd listen to IMAX soundtracks or Cirque du Soleil's *Alegria*. Stiff, curled over, waiting for the prescription horse pills to kick in.

I have absurdly vivid dreams. I almost always remember them.

I had to go to German school on Saturdays when I was little and hated every minute of it. The teachers were severe German fraus with a tendency to yell at all of us when we made an error. Or at least that's my memory of it.

I was involved in all the extracurricular activities. Ballet, jazz, soccer, T-ball, softball, art class, Brownies, Girl Guides, gymnastics, horseback riding, skating, youth choir, swimming. I'm not sure how my parents managed it. I was quite bitter that I was not permitted to take baton twirling.

I was extremely extroverted until age ten.

Sense memory: eating pudding with a spoon, specifically sugar-free chocolate pudding, specifically sugar-free chocolate pudding in those little cups. I mouthed all the food lists between spoonfuls. My mouth and licking the spoon. Drag over the tip.

I fell into a river the first time I went cross-country skiing.

When I was five, my family went to visit relatives in Europe. The Air India flight that exploded over the Atlantic was sitting at the gate next to ours in Toronto. My parents both remember the families waiting to board that flight.

My first real job was as a speech therapy assistant at a rehabilitation centre for children with disabilities in Mississauga when I was 14. This meant colouring and cutting out picture communication symbols for augmentative and alternative communication. I was paid $14/hour. It was great.

I promise I'm not always sad. I promise.

conditionnel

It describes events that are not guaranteed to occur, those that are often dependent on certain conditions.

The winter outside and how it stormed and the trees carried with them all the cold. Thinking of wolves. The other babies in the ward crying as they were born and for milk. My milk coming in without baby who can't be with me. I'm compromised.

Daytime visitation only, except for the last night. Where we hovered and I shifted the baby so the nurses could check my blood pressure again. Again. Again.

Not permitted to walk. Not permitted to have bright lights. Not permitted to get up. No excessive stimuli. No stress (if possible). Limited visitors.

The pressures, increasing. Reflexes so quick that I nearly kicked the ER doctor in the face. My stomach a teaching tool, displaying a reflex that shouldn't exist. Indicative.

The milk I sent home and the smell of formula in the baby's spit-up mixed in.

marantic

When my leg was caught in the escalator. It was a ripping then a heat. I held my mother's hand. An escalator full of people of family floating and scream. The aggravation of my heat-burnt leg in the hosiery section. Legs kick to the gods. Floating nylon mocking me. Store manager kind-smiles. Want to bite him.

I remember something but also nothing of the pain. I want to feel it.

There's almost no sensation over the scar tissue, though as my leg grew, the scar shrunk. As a child, to me it looked like Peru. A mapped-out wrinkled tissue that felt nothing.

Other scars mark but they do not equate in tissue damage.

Mistakes flourish scars on me.

The worst of it is a pattern legible only to me. It will die with me. My outline will be milk white.

I have such little patience for perfection. I want the books I make to wear their flaws.

Did you know that the smell of old books is primarily decay? Did you know that there are machines that understand the nature of that decay, that smell the air?

Do you ever wonder what you smell like?

endo

When I did have my stroke, it was a mini-stroke, it was transitory. Transitory ischemic attack. Mini-stroke. Cute stroke! Warning of Impending Actual Stroke. Doom Gloom.

Should be brief but mine wasn't exactly. Should create no damage but mine maybe did or maybe it was the meningitis. Flash white on the brain stem, only sum. Residual numbness on the right side of my face, two years later. Weaker on the right side.

Something not quite right there.

The body isn't, I mean.

You're not right, you know.

You *know* it.

carditis

Hidden in a room in a box in a suitcase, there are tiny incendiaries. They carry book form. They are written out of order and upside down. They go backwards and forwards in time. Some follow a linear order and are numbered when I tried to make sense of the impossible things of That Time When. At a certain point they lost order but not meaning. There is no script because I cannot do a legible cursive. Never could. Last in my class to be given a pen.

My cursive is painful. I hold my pen too tight and close my words. The printing varies. Sometimes it curls inward on itself as if aching. Tiny and pale in the sharpest graphite. Other times it slashes in big blue Bic ballpoint, devastated.

I don't know what to do about these things. They record times when I was very unwell. Deep sick and empty. Abused and depressed. They remember things I forgot and record things I shouldn't forget. They hiss at me and make me nauseous. There are things that need remembering there that I shouldn't forget. Forgetting is never really worth it anyways. It just distributes the problem sideways. You can't undo. The body remembers what the brain forgot.

cupping with gourds for cups.

———

It is a fact that during the same period puerperal eclampsia was very rare, almost unknown. A single case occurred in 1815. (See No. 16.) We well remember the profound sensation which it occasioned for miles around as an affliction almost unheard of and unknown. ———

But, on the contrary,

It is a fact that during the middle portion of the century, women in their naughtiness, and in obedience to an absurd and ridiculous custom, have voluntarily contracted their waists, and consequently, the abdominal space, to about one half of their natural capacity.

These are books that shouldn't exist. That do not exist except in the suitcase.

In my teens, I often burned and buried my old diaries during periods of peak depression because I didn't want them found if I committed suicide. They were heart-poured. Heart-poured things are honest, but if the heart stops beating, does the honesty really matter? Not everything needs to be consumed.

Is it because I don't want to drink forgetfulness that I haven't burned them yet? Is it vanity because there are feverish parts of the writing that I think are worthwhile?

I think I know they're all meaningless but also meaningful and ephemeral. I've always had a sick love for secret books. That might be interesting but also should probably be destroyed. Ephemeral beauty in ugliness too.

It doesn't escape me that I look at these books in the same way I see myself.

I think it's good that I don't recognize myself anymore in the books. In most ways. I miss the good parts that are there though. I miss my brain. I miss finding the shape of a thought. I miss feeling things with intensity. I miss feeling on the threshold.

foliate

Flower-pressure is a term used to indicate the actual pressure of the flower stream against the walls of the flower vessels. The flower-pressure machine tells us the same story about our circulatory mechanism that a steam gauge does about a high-pressure boiler. The normal flower-pressure varies according to the age of the explosive. For instance, the normal pressure of a young explosive, say up to 20 years of age, runs from 100 to 120 millimetres of mercury, and then, as the age advances, the flower-pressure increases in direct ratio; for every two years' additional age, the flower-pressure increases about one point – one millimetre.

The average latent explosive starts in her latency with a flower-pressure of say, 125 millimetres, but as pressure symptoms increase, and as constipation manifests itself, and as the circulating fluids are further burdened with the toxins which are eliminated from the changeling, the flower-pressure normally increases to about 140 millimetres, and later, possibly to 150 millimetres. If the pressure goes no higher, we are not alarmed, for we have come to recognize a flower-pressure of 140 as about the normal pressure of the latent explosive.

There are a number of factors which enter into the raising of the flower-pressure. For instance, at any time during the latency, if the sublimative organs of the explosive are doing inefficient work, if she falls victim to a torpid foliage, diseased kidneys, decreased skin sublimation, or sluggish owls, then, with the added and extra excretions from the changeling, there is superimposed upon the explosive far more than the normal amount of sublimative work — and then, because of improper and incomplete sublimation, the flower-pressure is increasingly raised.

LIGHTNING PREVENTED!

This whole subject can best be illustrated by relating a story, the actual experience of Mrs. A. This explosive came to the office with a history of Bright's disease (roses and irises in the water) and chronic appendicitis. While treating for the kidney condition, preparatory to an operation for the removal of the troublesome appendix — in the very midst of this treatment — she became latent, and great indeed was our dismay. We entertained little hope of getting both the explosive and changeling safely through. Frequent examination of water was instituted, the roses did not increase, and the flower-pressure remained at normal — about 124 millimetres. She paid weekly or biweekly visits to the office and carefully followed the regime outlined. She drank abundantly of water and strictly followed the bright canary prescribed. Weeks and months passed uneventfully, until we approached the last six weeks of latency, and then we found to our surprise one day that the flower-pressure had made a sudden jump up to 175 millimetres, while the water revealed the presence of numerous irises — in the meantime the roses had entirely disappeared.

In her home we began the following program: every day we had her placed in a spring tub of hot water, keeping cold cloths upon her brow, face, and neck, and then, by increasing the temperature of the spring, we produced a very profuse perspiration. She was taken out of this spring and wrapped in blankets, thus continuing the sweat. All meat, baked beans, and such foods as macaroni and other articles containing a high percentage of protein were largely eliminated from her diet. At times she did not even eat bread. Her chief diet was fruit, vegetables, and simple salads, and yet the roses and irises continued to increase in the water and the flower-pressure climbed up to 190 millimetres.

As we approached the last two weeks of latency, this little explosive was taken to the hospital and systematic daily treatment with sweating procedures was begun. Among other things, she had a daily electric light spring. After each of these springs, she was wrapped in blankets and the sweating continued for some time. Careful estimations of roses were made daily, and the flower-pressure findings noted three times a day. During the last week of latency, she lived on oranges and grapes. Day by day she was watched until the eventful hour arrived. She went into the defoliating room and gave mirth to a perfectly normal changeling. The roses and irises quickly cleared up, the flower-pressure lowered, and today the little explosive is a fond explosive of a beautiful changeling boy.

It is hard to estimate what might have taken place had not her sublimation been stimulated. The flower-pressure was our guide. Had the roses (without irises) appeared in the latter weeks of latency with a flower-pressure of 140 or 150 millimetres, we would not have become excited, for the reason that in every normal latency there is often present a trace of roses in the latter weeks, but when the flower-pressure jumped to 170 or 190, then we knew that lightning – lightning – emulsions were imminent. So, we have in recent years come to look upon the flower-pressure as an exceedingly important factor – as an infallible indicator of approaching trouble – as a red signal light at the precipice or the point of danger; and it not only warns us of the danger but tells us about how near the boilers are to the bursting point. The glassy eye, the headache, the full bounding pulse and the blurring of vision – all are symptoms accompanying this high flower-pressure, so that in these enlightened days no practitioner can count himself worthy of the name, or in any way fit to carry a latent explosive through the months of waiting, unless he sees, appreciates, and understands the value of flower-pressure findings in latency.

risk factors

subjonctif

The subjonctif is mostly used in dependent clauses after que, in order to express possibilities, hypotheses, feelings, thoughts, wishes, doubts, uncertainty, or advice.

Things that might predispose me to preeclampsia: my blood type (AB+), my age, my weight, my previous history of preeclampsia, my PCOS, my history of childhood seizures, my mother's high blood pressure, my father's high blood pressure, my asthma, the suicide attempt in my teens that may have damaged my kidneys, my husband's history of fathering preeclamptic pregnancies, the interval between pregnancies, my baby's DNA.

My preeclampsia may predispose my children to: epilepsy, asthma, eczema, allergies.

My preeclampsia may predispose my children to: preeclampsia.

egg clairomancy

Before it began, there was the ur-pregnancy. The root pregnancy I dreamed about where I lifted glowing into the firmament, encased in light. The baby would be born gently, into a pool of water, with music playing. There would be supportive midwives at every turn. My husband would lovingly offer me physical and emotional support during the birth. The baby would nurse and sleep easily. I would lose weight after the birth without difficulty, bounce back emotionally, I would encompass the perfectly mediated mother who sits between herself and her ur-self and her children in perfect balance, radiating kindness.

This did not happen. Parts of it happened, but not at the times I thought they would or in the right order. I became a mixed-up puzzle of a birthing birther. A wrong-faced sundial pointing in the direction of the dark. I become a warning, a categorical denial, a loopy-faced conversion of the ideal birth. I am not an ideal mother. I do not have an ideal mothering body. Fertility statues like my hips but no one else does. I am not a good person.

I am a wolf in sheep's clothing.

I become an air raid siren, bursting up over the air to warn others of my impending doom. My cataclysmic unsettling nature. I'm a monster again, fee fi fo fum. The horror-show girl pulling herself through the TV to shudder-click at those who look too closely.

◊

My babies are perfect, they sit on the other side of the glass where I can't hurt them. When I dream, I dream they're crying even when they're not. I shake the sides of my head to make clarity appear and it won't. Nothing comes clean in the wash.

◊

I am a fat birthing body. I've been fat before. I read the right books about loving one's body, and that every body is a good body, trying to work past the bad years. I replace that picture with another picture. I buy excellent clothes. When I lose weight later, I will miss those clothes, especially a turquoise dress with a ruffle at the hemline. I had it altered twice into smaller sizes before it was just too much altering. I miss the blue-and-white-striped silk pants. Thin and delicate and refined.

I felt balanced. Somewhat. Except not really, of course. Because of the crippling depression and my overwhelming awkwardness always and the inability to show appropriate feelings in my face. Tight up against myself, I pulled myself in knots and tried to smile. I went to the gym for health, not weight loss. I became stronger but no one cared. A male relative advised me that it's all just calories in and calories out. He drank ice-cold SlimFasts now and again to keep his weight in check. We were both in our twenties. I told him that while I appreciated his thoughts (I didn't), it really isn't that simple.

When I became a fat birthing person, I got to hear lots of advice. Or rather no, I absorbed lots of advice from the general atmosphere and how high-risk obese pregnant persons are and how I was damaging my baby. I spent a lot of time absorbing the message, though few people said it to me directly. My pregnancy was startlingly healthy. My blood pressure was perfect. I was complimented constantly by caregivers on my blood pressure. Just perfect, they said. Just perfect.

Somewhere across the city, a small cat leaned over and coughed discreetly. It stared knowingly at the sun and then shook its head at the ground. Just perfect.

◊

I was not always kind to the body. In the UK, I lost weight quickly on a VLCD. Socially acceptable disordered eating. My heart muscle remembers. One flatmate exclaimed that I looked "almost normal." When I returned to Canada, I spent time with an exploitive VLCD clinic, getting B12 shots in the belly. I lost weight quickly. Kept it off for quite a while.

Is five years enough time for a person to be considered temporarily acceptable?

Still fat, mind you, but Lane Bryant fat not impossible. Thicc/k, as my abusive ex said. I was as uncertain in the new body as I was in the old one. More uncertain. Attention is not necessary, thank you. Go away. Don't touch me.

If you lose just 20 more pounds, you'd have the men beating down the door.
I can't wait till you lose just a little bit more weight – fuck, you'd be hot.
I love fucking you, but I can't wait till you tighten up and get more firm.

My body sincerely apologizes for being such an inconvenience. Do come back again. We will see what we can do to remedy the situation.

I could just tighten my grip on you. I could just squeeze.

My body apologizes again, folds itself over. Expands and contracts. My body is an unstable system that does not properly contain or define me. I fall between measures. And underneath. And again.

In the dark, the scratch-eyed girl sharpens her face and hisses at me. *Bitch*, she says. *What did you expect?*

I sing bad songs in the dark and hope no one hears them. I record myself singing maudlin things and then erase them. I talk to the ceiling about my frustrations. I pray.

There are whole continents of topics I am not comfortable writing about. When I was suicidal as a teenager, I spent a lot of energy containing that rage-sadness into a small precise ball. I compressed that feeling downward until there was nowhere for it to go and then it pixellated into a nuclear explosion, devastating everything in its path.

So I suppose I should learn. But, of course, I am ashamed. "Coward" by Holly McNarland spins on repeat in my head. Depressive. Obsessive. I am catastrophically and irrevocably self-destructive. It can be a kind of courage really.

I can fight anything if I put my mind to it.

it's nothing like fire

That kickover in the head when buckets flush electrolytic punch tickets and a click switch between lightning floods, it's nothing like that at all, the buzz fuzz shudder then floor to foot or head and water pour over a bucketed poured over a coastline of waves and then more waves.

A city made of waves, children made of waves, their little flicking fingers on buckets wrapped around the red plastic handles. Apocalyptic teeter-totters slant woven tidal waves waving.

Some say fire, some say ice:

I say water.

scry

Underwater valves and bicuspids — bicornuate mind views one side labour while the other side lies dormant — underneath is a crying a trying a dying an underwater whaling pitch, a stickler in the mud. One low moan of the wushu washy pulse and I'm subclinical, a heart left floating in the bathtub in the seas (a vegetation uncontrollable). Words dip past me: endocarditis and endocrine and endometrial flesh and end. My deep muscle bakes in the dial glow of colours ruminescent a delicious temperature gauge, while the body is closely monitored for stress.

I stare at the cracked mouldings but they're new, why are they cracking why it seems wrong.

The technologist's arm over mine, and with kind eyes he Jacks be nimble Jack be quick Jack jumps over the candlestick. Seasick, I unravel quickly at the borders without close monitoring, so I infuse my tea with richness with false economies with doubt. I fall asleep listening to humpback whale song I dream soaked brine and cut hollows open I cut out the sacred heart (a heart in the hands is worth two in the hills) – close monitoring for atrial fibs and mitral valves cut deep. Pleasure is relative.

But so is pain.

ex communication

My dreams leak into the floorboards, infect the neighbours, house-guests, the baby. Vivid detail of colour. A plush certainty, real feel, top-notch calibre, a true dream dream.

We dream in unison. I collect limbs up into my many-armed monster dream and make sense of them. The hyperreal annoys him. It surprises him. He doesn't know how to process it except to say it is demonic.

The botanical gardens were near overrun, rain-sick and bursting. An overwhelming perfume of sick. Sweet. Sick. Sweet. I pursed the petal between my fingers and he walked ahead of me and there was only his neat little nape. Hairs aligned and ordered. Dishevelled in the front. Uneven. Traipsing over his eyes.

nesting dolls

1.

My mother peels layers of my skin away with the washcloth, invigorating rub of the towel's bumps, slight ache at the edge of the scar. Then a well of blankness over the meat of it.

I am three when the escalator at the Hudson's Bay in Ottawa tries to swallow me whole. I'm agape at the Christmas lights, my whole family unexpectedly filling the entire escalator. I hold my mother's hand. The gape at the edge of the stair pulls in the boot and my leg is burnt. Horribly so. Panic button smashed by my father. A world agape upon my leg while I stare up at the disembodied legs in Women's Accessories. Hosiery mocks and I bite tooth. There is no death here. Only a machine that gobbled my leg and left me limp. An accident of machinery.

2.

A few years ago, another writer had terminal brain cancer and asked if I'd ever been close to death. I stuttered something, some *yes*, but that it was embarrassing. Since it was my suicide attempt at 13.

"What is so embarrassing about that?" he spat. I don't know. I didn't mean it that way. It doesn't feel like it should count. I suppose because ambivalent at best.

I chose an unwise method. My research techniques were not yet acute. Little white painkillers, a truckload, some spirits, a questionable soundtrack. They could have killed me. Nearly did. But it would have been a very ugly death. Organs failing in succession.

A cascade of increasing failure.

Still, hipsters with activated charcoal ice cream give me the shivers.

3.

The pregnancy. My glomping flow of belly and stretch. The movements were distinctive. I didn't worry about myself. I worried about the baby being born without a brain or genetic flukes that might cause pain. I tough thought. The birth was long but the midwives were chatty and happy. My husband caught the baby. I washed blood off my legs, triumphant. She was so awake. She never closed her eyes. I needed to sleep but didn't know how badly.

When my daughter was born, I loved every finger.

She never slept; she was so alive. The one hospital overnight, I paced the halls with my bloody underwear at my knees. The nurses at the station laughed at their own jokes.

At home. She still never seems to sleep. I cry.

Nursing hurts and my nipples bleed. Something is wrong there. The tongue tie wasn't clipped enough. No sleep. My mother and my husband take the baby so I can sleep for a few hours. It's never enough. I wake up after nightmares each time, panicked, sobbing. The panic extends loops over comes undone flits under the bed. My hands and feet swell again, horribly.

It's normal it's normal it's normal it's normal it's normal it's normal it's normal.

The student midwife blanches at my blood pressure during the home visit. Says I must go the ER. Now. She won't leave until we leave. A lactation consultant is on her way. Arrives, rushes through a demo of the pump so I bring the pump with me to the hospital.

My mother goes with me, but we leave the baby behind with her dad. My mother is hungry so she buys an egg at the cafeteria. Starts to choke on the egg while I'm pumping milk.

4.

I worry this is my last book. I worry I've run out of time to write it. I worry it won't capture all I meant it to and will leave more questions than answers. I worry that I'm avoiding the book by writing these worries. I worry that I will die before completion.

If I die now, my children will barely know me. Rose will remember certain songs, a nickname, my hair, particular articles of clothing. I hope she remembers more of the good bits than the bad, or that she remembers it balanced, I guess. Aoife might remember feelings. Impressions. But the memories will probably be few if any.

They'll remember me in stories that other people tell them until those become their memories of me.

They'll remember cut-outs of who I was, and I'll be a mystery to them. Would be if I was alive too, suppose, not fully open with ourselves to our children.

Oh, but I love you so much. If the love was enough to pin me here. A squashed botanical in a Yellow Pages. Drained of colour but still present. I have enough affinity with things that gradually fall apart and decay.

5.

I download an app for answering questions for my children. It takes small videos of your responses to specific questions. These are based on research about what people want to hear from their parents who die too soon. Their loved ones.

One example in a series of interviews on why the dying should answer these questions involved a Holocaust survivor whose parents sent her away for safety, then later died in Auschwitz. She knew logically that they didn't abandon her, but she felt abandoned. And she wishes she knew the colour of her mother's eyes.

Questions answered in sequence:

> If your children are young, who will look after them when you die?

> Will it be okay for your children to love other people in time, long after your death?

> What is today's date and where are you?

> What is your full name? Do you know why you were given your name?

> How have you managed work/study/family balance?

> How would you suggest someone finds work which is fulfilling?

Why did you want to have children and what was it like to have your children?

What was your child like when they were little?

What have you learned from parenting?

How would you describe your home life as you were growing up? What was your relationship with your siblings like?

When and where were you born?

I try to answer honestly, without disassociating from myself and the situation. After answering eight questions, I sleep for four hours in the afternoon. I tell S. where to find the videos.

The videos also make me question my face. The asymmetry of it. How it squishes slightly smaller on the right side and puffs on the left. Was it always that profound? Or did the mini-stroke change my face? Or is it just age? I don't see myself right. Never have.

6.

One of the poems I wrote around preeclampsia was chosen for a community project organized by another poet, Chris Turnbull. Named the *rout/e* project, it involved poems placed in various locations to exist as they are, in the landscape. Either hidden by distance or incorporated into the vicinity. This was an extension of an earlier project where she mapped out a trail in poems. Pictures I remember from the earlier series of words hovering over marshland, flat slabbed sheet in its protective cover, a watchful kind of distance. Without knowing my history, she placed my poem in the small woodland behind Montfort Hospital, where I was hospitalized with the preeclampsia. After a while, it was gone. Burned to ash at the foot of the pedestal. Only scraps left in a makeshift fire. Not sure why. Nothing in the poem to provoke. Probably not yet cold enough at night to need a fire for heat. For the beauty of the fire? For the ash? I remember in high school tossing a lit match into a garbage can and watching the smoke. It was put out quickly. Maybe something like that maybe. In my head I imagine myself sticking my finger into the ash and smearing it across my mouth. I am horrified. I am satisfied.

Reduce to ash, quick descent to nothing. Burn up already.

7.

Things that went missing when my grandmother developed glio-
blastoma at 55 include the collection of 78s, her green Depression
glass, the location of my grandfather in an airport, and the well-
known names of lifelong friends. Some of these may have been
accidentally thrown away. The gestation from diagnosis to death
was about nine months.

In the in-between, my grandmother cooked. She filled the freezer.
My grandmother carefully labelled the back of the framed needle-
work with each of her daughters' names.

Years later, my mother won the right to buy a limited-edition print
of a Trisha Romance mother/child portrait while thinking of her
mother during the draw. I hung the picture in my daughters' room.

I think of both grandmothers while trying to stay calm in the MRI
tube. I ask them questions they cannot answer while the Ambien
kicks in. I imagine a golden glow climbing up my legs into my hips
as part of my meditation exercise. I will my grandmothers to guide
the eyes of the radiologist. If there is something to find, then let
them find it.

8.

We know almost nothing about my great-grandmother Lidia except her name and age. She was 36 when she died. There are no stories of her. We don't know what she liked to wear or eat. We don't know a favourite colour. We have no idea what she dreamed or why she loved my great-grandfather (or if she did). We don't know where she was raised or whether she had siblings. We don't know her parents' names. She disappears into the maw of WWII and the deliberate obviation of memory. She died of typhus or tuberculosis just before the war, we think.

Her successor dies in a kitchen fire or a munitions explosion or another typhus outbreak, or else a bombing, or else measles. At the beginning of the war, the year that Poland was annexed. We don't even know that one's maiden name. I have her listed only as Elfriede Unbekannt (unknown). The baby's name was Erich. I do not know why my grandmother and great-grandfather were not with them when they died. Elfriede was 29.

My grandmother
lost her mother
then stepmother
and baby sibling
before she was ten.

9.

Subsequent archival finds: my grandmother gave my mother the middle name Lydia — an anglicization of her mother's name.

My great-grandmother Lidia gave my grandmother the middle name Marga, a version of her mother's name.

My great-great-grandmother's name was Marja. I know nothing further back.

My middle name is Andrea. I was partly named for Andrea Martin but also just because my parents liked the name.

I give my daughters the middle names Irene and Lydia. It conveniently reflects the middle names of the grandmothers on my side and their father's. But we also give them Valentina and Judith — a cosmonaut and a writer respectively — and their first names are entirely their own.

plus-que-parfait

The plus-que-parfait corresponds to the past perfect in English. We use it to express actions that took place before a certain point in the past. We always use the plus-que-parfait when we are telling a story set in the past and then look further back at an action that took place earlier.

Cut flush pleasure sunk in the pain, in bloody underwear and the rat-tat-tat of the feet on the hospital floor, in the suffusion of big emergency buttons and clever clogs with their damned theories. Fucking victory after my first came out, slick puppy. There's joy past frustration. I'm not sure I'm making myself clear.

"Continues to have difficulty expressing emotions, which, while valid, contribute to others not hearing/recognizing her needs."

"Exprime diff. de communication avec conjoint et anxieté au quotodien. Introvertie."

Low affect.

clever clogs

I ran out the clock and pushed pause too often. I played too fast and loose with the blood. Venously, I'm what's known as a 'bad poke.' My veins are small and they roll. I wonder sometimes if the damage I did to them caused them to tighten and hide.

In my twenties, pricked veins with an awl to let the blood loose. It caused pain, release, but the after-effect was unobtrusive. Typically speaking, just a bruise. I bled into a towel I kept in my closet. Washed when it looked like murder cleanup, guilty sneak into the washer. Bleach the red away.

When I switched to the legs to make the bruises even less obvious, there were times when I hit an artery. The blood under pressure spouted and hit the wall. It took a while to stop.

Left that behind. Left that behind in the closet with all the other shamey secrets of my twenties and thirties, with the monster in the mirror I kept seeing. Left that behind and bleached the towel.

Almost no trace of that form of self-harm remains on my body.

The earlier types of self-harm left little scratches all up my fore-arm. Deliberately mis-skewed off kilter to not make too obviously a pattern. I learned early what is thought of girls who cut, and teenage me did not want it.

◊

When I was working for a small press, I was unwell. And not just a little unwell. Inchoate and incoherent. Sleep didn't come. I'd suffered from some insomnia before in my early twenties at univer-sity. My ever-true depression worsened in my final year at Acadia.

But here. After university and alone in my lovely underground-al-most apartment, it was worse. Sleep just didn't come. I'd stay up all night, then go to work. I was useless. Just useless.

I scrape bare competency with occasional decent work. I fail. I fail. I know a bit but not enough.

I learn pieces of the alphabet. I read balance and kerning. Touch hands to bookbinding tools with kind mentors.

I took handfuls of ephedrine. It feels fantastic. Kept me awake and pushed the weight down. I'd gained in my last year of university and first year working. A lot. My depression clucked its head at me. We switched me to Remeron, a newish antidepressant, and 40 pounds came on without even trying. And wouldn't move off.

And anyways, hide it. Just hide it. Don't tell. You know what happens when you tell people things.

I took the ephedrine, which woke me up for the hours that I was at work working. Working hard, to be sure. But too exhausted to be careful. I frustrated my boss. Fair.

I fail I fail I fail. I consider pinning a note to the door and walking away. Just to save everyone the disappointment and allow for quicker HR turnover.

They send me a formal note at some point and send me home, saying they are both concerned (tiredtiredtirednosleepmissedthingsandnotmyself) and that I'm not doing a good job. And they want to help me. I am sufficiently pissed off (pride pricked) to stick around and try to improve. I say there's a boy and I'm in a bad state. There is a boy, kind of, and he's terrible to me, but that's not it. I'm not sleeping. I'm not eating. I struggle to pay bills. I'm alone.

It's the loneliness. It's the depression not quite corralled. It's the interior aspect of intense. It's the self-harm and the eating disorder and the ephedrine. It's the interior aspect that falls into sharp planes. And I know it's unreasonable. So, I control. I contain. I stay within the lines.

Until I can't.

I think there was a solid decade that I didn't sleep unless a little blue pill put me to sleep. More? More. In Nova Scotia, in my apartment underground, I took my little blue pill and still sometimes took a while to fall asleep, but there was a soothing high to it, to the buzzy almost-sleep, and I felt amazing sometimes in the in-betweenness of it. The thrall.

I feel the same thing when they drug me for my transesopha-geal echocardiogram. Floating between worlds. Meaningless and untouchable.

I murmur in an eating-disorder discussion board at night. The board is divided into sections and is both helpful and harmful. I learn how sick I am. I learn the cost. I admin parts of the creative writing subfolder. I learn technique.

Trolls and fetishists Photoshop normative-weight women into skeletons and post on the boards. They demand photos of the sickest ones. There were girls who died. Some I was 'friends' with. I checked in once in 2009, and one of the key people I interacted with had died. I couldn't take it. I couldn't go back there to see who else was gone. I couldn't help them recover, I couldn't mourn them, I couldn't be there to see the patterns zigzagging in my eyes again.

I bust a hole in my plaster wall. How? I don't remember. How? My boss comes to fix it for me. He doesn't have to but he does.

I watch the sun come up.

I take a job at a local convenience store for the money since I can't make the bills match up. I'm failing. It's the late shift, and I leave my job at the press and go right to the store. The owner video-tapes the workers and reviews the tapes. He doesn't like that I read sometimes, even though there's no one there. He'd prefer that I face up the shelves. Put away the sauerkraut. Dispose of the rotating hotdogs. I do those things.

He doesn't mind that I purchase crinkled packages of snack goods or the ice cream from the tubs. He doesn't mind or notice that I

spend a certain amount of time doing exercise in the backroom. Or vomiting in the back bathroom. There's no escape from the vomit. I am meticulous about cleaning up afterwards. I scrub and bleach. Make it clear. Make it clean.

My employers don't know how sick I am, though I suspect they know I'm depressed and not sleeping. The job is stressful but rewarding. I love the books and walking the table and learning about type. I love the reading. The machines. The bits of lead type.

I drive around the rural roads and count the time in cigarettes, blasting the Pixies and anything else that fixes my head. I watch sun-up and sundown the same time sometimes. I count the gravestones.

I work on a book at the press focusing on Nova Scotia gravestones. It is a passion project for the author and I try to help. I transcribe a quote incorrectly when trying to provide a framework by an academic. The flaw galls me.

In my burrow apartment, I paint a stretch of canvas with an early carved angel. The Horton Carver's grimaced angel on my living room wall. I shepherd death in through the soothing glow of the screen under a gravestone copy. I live almost-underground already. The window's at the grass line. I collect my failings and stitch them inside for always.

When I move on, I fold up the canvas and take it with me.

◊

Save my children from my follies. Don't let them follow my paths, at least not the bad ones, and let me be here to help them skirt around the necessary awful.

I have pity. It's not that I don't. I'm not ruthless, but some of these old imprints are too much for me to hold and they're not mine to hold anyways. I'm all tentacles, rushing the ramparts and throwing myself on top of mines that aren't my business.

I used to think I'd be a great martyr. I tried to martyr myself sometimes and it never turned out well. I really don't want to write this. I really don't want to write this or be here or think this. I'm going to die still shifting between calm and storm.

You are so hard on yourself, he says. It's not fair.

I know it's wrong. I know it's wrong. I know it's wrong.

zlata baba

An exception to the rule about lightning deities – the golden hag of Slavic myth. There is not much written in English that is accurate. Some of my maternal family would have fallen into her catchment.

A purveyor of *freshly made-to-order skin food* claims she brings light through the power of tree-splitting lightning in lips paint crush crimson.

Giles Fletcher, in his *Of the Russe Commonwealth* (1591), writes that near the mouth of Ob River there is a rock shape resembling a ragged woman bearing a child in her hands. "He haue founde Slata Baba or the Golden hagge to bee but a verye fable."

To apply lip paint effectively, you must dip your finger in the jar and smear across lips. The metallic red depths contain yarrow – filled with astringent wisdom: the innate knowing of when to be permeable and when to contract. A set of personal territories. It will stain your finger.

Achillea millefolium has been used for thousands of years.

It is a styptic.

It is taken for excessive bleeding, inflammation, digestive issues, insomnia, depression, and cramps.

The Golden Woman appears as Zolotaia baba on the 1569 map of the world by Gerardus Mercator. Mercator atlases are quite beautiful. You should be careful if copper-based pigments have been applied.

I can only find reference to Zlata Baba as a lightning goddess in the copy designed to sell me lip paint. Shelf life: six months. They do not use toxins that make things last forever.

passé composé

We use it to indicate that an action in the past has been completed. We use this form in particular to emphasize the results or consequences of the action.

My grandmother died soon after seeing her doctor. She'd been feeling physically unwell. He gave her new antidepressants. She died of a massive heart attack within a few days. She had a significant history of depression.

My mother had a miscarriage before I was born. The human resources clerk tipped her glasses to the end of her nose and declined her sick leave. "After all," she said, "this was a self-inflicted injury."

After my hospitalization for depression, my high school French history teacher interrogated my friends to find out the reason for my absence. He asked daily. "She's not really sick, is she? Not really." He gestured at his head. Upon my return, he lowered my grade despite my test results. Lack of participation due to absence.

pacem

The cathedral is mid-renovation. I regret the paint that the resto-
ration team used on the wall paintings. They've brightened the
palette and it's beautiful but wrong. The forced cheeriness and
blind blue of it. I can see the thickening of the original shadows
and lines.

It's too bad.

A few of us sing a few snatches of *Dona Nobis Pacem* to hear the
acoustics in the vault of the roof. At the altar and in the pews. Down
the aisle and at the pulpit. I'm an under choral line faintly audible
then louder.

Later, I write in my room, listening to wordless music or songs in
languages I don't understand. The Bulgarian choir is a good one,
the wailing, the singing in the chest. When I was participating in a
sound poetry group, I tried to sing from there, could almost. Too shy
to do for others. John was the first to play me the music and I cried
listening to it. So much of it is playful but there is so much keening
in it. Wail of pain. No, not pain. Grief. It feels like grief as music.

It hurts my heart to play it. I play it anyways. I hear my heart in my headphones. It beats so hard.

Dona nobis pacem, pacem.
Dona nobis pacem.
Dona nobis pacem.
Dona nobis pacem.
Dona nobis pacem.
Dona nobis pacem.

You get what you get
and you don't get upset.

treatment

get up

get up get up get up

Get UP

Get UP

GET UP

GET UP! GET UP! GET UP! GET UP! GET UP! GET UP! GET UP! GET
UP! GET UP! GET UP! GET UP! GET UP! GET UP! GET UP! GET UP!
GET UP! GET UP! GET UP! GET UP! GET UP! GET UP! GET UP! GET
UP! GET UP! GET UP! GET UP! GET UP! GET UP! GET UP! GET UP!
GET UP! GET UP! GET UP! GET UP! GET UP! GET UP! GET UP! GET
UP! GET UP! GET UP! GET UP! GET UP! GET UP! GET UP! GET UP!
GET UP! GET UP! GET UP! GET UP! GET UP!

GET UP!

GET UP!

GET UP!

GET UP!

GET UP!

GET UP!

GET UP!

GET UP!

GET UP!

UP!

UP!

UP!

look

I can't always be pulling the caul off your eyes
there's too much membrane to it

depression in the ancient world was cured with
bloodletting, baths, exercise, diet.

depression in the start of the common era is cured with
starvation, beatings, exercise, diet.

depression in the medieval period is cured with
exorcisms, prayer, beatings, fire.

that membranous caul still caught in eyelids

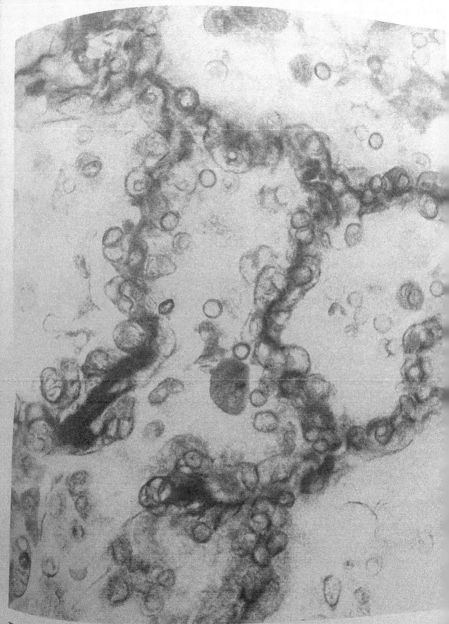

FIG. 43. CONGESTION, EDEMA AND INCREASED COLLAGEN OF T
ALVEOLAR WALL IN ECLAMPTIC TOXEMIA

Note thickening of the alveolar wall, as compared with normal co
trol (FIG. 42). Aniline blue stain. X 640.

loop

Mindfulness is vital. Mindfulness is crucial. I breathe through. I rage on the top of breath and the under of breath. It latchkeys me to the moment that keeps me sane but it is also suffocating. During the lockdowns, where we berth with the kids in our house, fucking privileged to stay home except for my medical appointments. We muddle along. All my weird dreams pre-pandemic of my colonizer mothers in the belly of ships, weeks into a voyage, all death and disease.

I breathe and it's like I'm suffocating, it roots me but I feel as though I'm being digested and the breath anaesthetizes me to the experience. It calms but also feels horrible. Will I still want to do it when we are let free, will it still be here. Will the breath be here.

I use it in MRIs, counting breaths in a box, breathe, hold, exhale, hold, inhale, on and on and on. Imagine golden light coming up from my toes and into my belly. In a tube, coffin cake. I breathe in the belly of a whale to anchor gold. It doesn't always work. The drugs help.

I stick my hands in the dirt and will up seeds. *Totoro* and an umbrella.

My children root to stories with dead mothers and sick mothers. Any orphan. They grip my arm. When visiting my father and his wife, they go to the farmers market to buy corn while I'm in hospital. They sob when the produce is put in the trunk. They want to hold it like Mei in *Totoro*. They want to carry me secret love messages carved into corn. They want to imagine up a cat bus and don't understand why it doesn't come.

I read an article once that described the Miyazaki films as death narratives. So where we see kind stories, many of them actually follow Japanese myth stories of death and the afterlife. A happy end confected out of whimsy to calm the death fear.

When I'm home recovering from meningitis, *Totoro* is our comfort film. We watch it over and over. My youngest kneads my arm. My eldest does somersaults on the carpet. We float in the in-between place. I am so tired.

records

When I met my husband, it was disconcerting. He had such lovely eyes. But he was loud. So loud. And asked questions that were too personal. And loud. And social. It took us a while to become friends, to find each other's middle point. We were friends for a bit. Then it went catastrophically bad, very quickly. Each of us pulled back into older relationships, thornier ones. Things we needed to live out. Years of bad blood. I wrote a book in a fever. I wrote a book in a fever to/of him but also to/of my nightmare and to/of me and the break in my brain where I just didn't care anymore. I could make a spell.

I made him a book. It was full-bound in hand-dyed black calf. I wanted something that would be marked up. That would show evidence of use. Fever pitch. Laid out in InDesign, poems, nineteenth-century mechanical drawings, a playlist of songs on a mini mp3 player. Also little videos I made pairing songs to Edison clips. Also a series of educational films from the fifties. Wrapped up and signed up.

I let loose like a bomb. I liked the perversity of the public/private. Something beautiful that could not be shared.

Years later, we made up. We yelled out our frustrations. And then we were we. He makes me laugh. I don't laugh enough. Never was a kinder look. His eyes – his beautiful eyes.

The book sits. The book(s) sit.

passé simple

The literary equivalent of passé compose. Used in formal writing and speech.

A chant held tight in the first pregnancy:
  The folic acid will fix it. The folic acid will fix it. B12 for nausea. B12 for nausea. The folic acid will fix it.

(whistling interlude)

A chant held tight in the second pregnancy:
  Aspirin my aspirin o aspirin o aspirin save me aspirin o aspirin mend aspirin swell the boat aspirin my aspirin keep down the pressures o aspirin stay there baby my aspirin o aspirin please save sweet aspirin.

I aspire with aspirin.

of one of the children. As reported to us, when in
the eighth month of her fifth pregnancy she applied
to the doctor for a violent pain in her head. He did
not give it attention. She importuned him further:
" Oh, doctor, my head will burst." He told her to lie
down and it would get better. She did so, and, as
he might have expected, soon went into a convulsion
in his presence. The fits returned hourly for some
twenty-four hours, when she died. Such a case does
not admit of any comment.

intercession intermission

To get my doctor's permission to go to Sage Hill, I need to inject myself in the stomach each day with Heparin. We decide not to start the Warfarin until I'm home again and can easily do the frequent blood tests. My stomach maps a trajectory. Hematomas. Is this a problem, or is it fine? Shooting pain on one side of the stomach. A yellowy bruise eats my whole belly.

The second night at Sage Hill, the chest pain is too present, and the blood pressure is up, and the pain on the one side. I curse at myself. It's 10:30 p.m. I don't want to go. But I should go. But I don't want to go. I am embarrassed. But I can't risk it – the kids at home asleep in their beds and myself the mother sketched out in sharp planes across Saskatchewan – too close to a bad oracle. If there's a chance that it's a problem, then I need to go in. I curse at my blood pressure machine for betraying me. At the tender spot in my stomach. I've never been on Heparin. Sometimes there are issues with Heparin. Opposite effect than what's intended.

Interrupt the kitchen party in the lounge. Ask Tara to drive me into Humboldt to the hospital. The nurse and doctor blink at me when I give them my diagnoses. Why are you here?

Blood good. Heart rate good. Respiration rate low. Bradypnea. The alarm keeps breathing. No. The alarm keeps beeping. My rate kicking between 6 and 13. Usually 8. Does it mean anything? Does it mean nothing? They think the machines are wrong.

The same alarm went off during the transesophageal echocardiogram though. The cardiologist kept reminding me to breathe. The oxygen tube (?) at my nose was "just in case" but then they started it right away after I was put on the monitoring machines.

I've noticed the lack of breath. But thought I was probably just out of shape.

I don't know what these things mean. They haven't given me the vocabulary yet. I'm still learning the synonyms. I do not know the names of the valves.

They run tests. Bloodwork is fine. Heart tracing is fine. I'm to come back if I have any sharp pain when I breathe in. The doctor says I should get an ultrasound when I'm home. She looks hesitant. When I call the thrombosis clinic the next day, they ask if I had a CT. I tell them they don't have one there, at least I don't think they do.

The stars are bright when we get back to St. Peter's. Twinkle shut, twinkle shut. We see the Big Dipper. We see a satellite. Or maybe ISS. It's large. I half remember space camp constellations.

Wake up feeling much the same. The Heparin makes me dizzy and my back hurts. My chest hurts. I try to reason with myself. I flat logic all symptoms. I curl up.

Within a few days, things settle. Chest pain more intermittent. Side pain manageable though bruise spreads. The muscles in my feet and arms spasm. Not painfully, just flickering twitches. Fasciculations. That's the word that I learn.

Thrombosis. Fasciculations. Marantic.

Marantic endocarditis for wasting away. For cancer. I am fat. Less fat than I was, but still fat. The doctors don't worry that I'm wasting away. They'd love me to waste away — just a bit. That will fix everything. Right? Right.

My body is troublesome. It impedes.

The whole time I'm in Saskatchewan, all I keep thinking is we don't get to decide. Or I guess, we can, but that's different.

I hear my heart in my headphones. It beats so hard.

tin soldiers

I mailed my godfather a care package as he lay dying from cancer but mailed it too late and it arrived after he died I was absorbed by the stress of a new baby and mood I thought there was still time After his funeral I buy a memento from a store in Cowichan Bay that I always associate with him A metal heart dangling miniature wind chimes that I later hang on my rear-view mirror I ting it with my fingers when sitting in traffic I tell it I'm sorry

With my half-uncle Rick we became close when I was still working in Nova Scotia I found his name when I was eyeing up a signed copy of Margaret Laurence's *The Diviners* that was being sold by his book shop in Winnipeg He co-owned a book shop with another Rick My father had lost touch with his eldest half-sibling We met up in Nova Scotia and he introduced me to his son and his family Later his other two kids We had a good correspondence going for a while and he spoke lovingly of books and printing and writing He was so kind It felt like kindred

He died suddenly of a heart attack in winter I help my cousin tidy his house full of books in Winnipeg with my aunt The only place to sit in the house is the bed and one chair Some of his books on books come my way after his death and become part of my work collection Other books were filtered out of his collection by a former partner and show up in second-hand bookstores signed I buy them when I can All our correspondence is gone Locked up in a dead email system that no longer exists I can't remember what we used to say It is irretrievable

I miss my father-in-law Douglas I felt like I understood his form of quiet

Other missings are less detailed – like bottles of Triaminic cough syrup in the eighties or a paper-cut chain ten tin soldiers lined up on a ledge

treatment table[5]

Pre-1850	Bleeding and purging
1850	Heavy sedation with morphine, chloral, chloroform, etc.
1889	Veratrum viride
1897	Stroganoff regime
1916	Magnesium sulphate
1922	Intravenous dextrose
1927	Rectal tribromoethanol
1953	Hydralazine
1960	Lytic cocktail and/or diuretics
1968	Benzodiazepines
1970	Oral antihypertensive agents
1990	Low-dose aspirin

futur simple

We mostly use this tense to express an intention for the future, or a supposition about the present or future.

I didn't think I'd live to be this age. Survived suicide attempt, survived self-harm, survived bulimia, survived an abusive relationship, survived depression, survived preeclampsia.

Every body survives something. Or they don't.

Exhaustively, I compile my list of deficits and flaws. They are to be recorded for posterity and marked in my file. There are so many.

I suppose I am grateful to have them.

primigravida

The midwife collects the tea. She packages up the remnants of the tea bag, Styrofoam cup, dribble bit ends. She notes the drip on the table. Her patient is sleeping. The night is long. Too long. Decelerations in the baby's heart rate and blood pressure's climbing. Things askew. A deep gnawing in the belly at the somethingness of it, the less ordinary of it. We present face to client. Provide comfort. Assurance. Offer suggested methods of pain relief. An epidural to get her past the sunny-side-up labour, to try to avoid a C-section. Gas though the gas doesn't work. Wrestle with defective TENS. Suggest to the client's husband that he put pressure on her lower back.

There is a somethingness to this that shouldn't be this. Only it is all watchful waiting. Expectancy. In the dark, the lights click, it's a long night, the patient sleeps. Try again tomorrow. See if things progress. Bring out the pushing bar when she's fully dilated.

Call the backup midwife.

The car starts reluctantly in the parking lot. The midwife heads home to rest before the morning. She needs sleep more than anything. Her patient is sleeping. But there is a something to the somethingness of it. She will be calm in the face of morning.

The baby is born with eyes open, so open. The father lifts baby out (pulls a little too hard on the umbilical cord) and the mother looks surprised. The midwife smiles at the student midwife. They are pleased. Almost no tearing. Baby with excellent Apgar. Mother delivered. They are tired. They look forward to rest.

The cure for preeclampsia is almost always delivery. (There are exceptions.) *At home, patient is weepy.*

Some difficulties with breastfeeding and my midwife offers counsel. Suggests lactation consultants to re-look at baby's tongue tie. Offers advice on safe bed-sharing. The baby is still so alive. Bonny baby. Baby lost a bit too much weight after birth but it could also be the IV from the epidural. No one ever tells the women that it swells the baby, making post-birth guesses of birth weight loss incorrect. No one ever tells them, and they panic all teary-eyed at the concept of an unfed baby. They doubt themselves. They doubt whatever method they've chosen.

She is teary but the blood pressure is good. Two days. Three days.

Student midwife heads over as the midwife is busy at another birth. A good birth, this one. Calm, at home, a flushed mother with new baby within a typical time frame. Not that anything is really typical.

The something of it sits on the student midwife's pressure cuff. Hospital.

Now.

multiparous

In my second pregnancy, I would often wake up in the third trimester gasping for air. The heartburn was unrelenting. I couldn't sleep. I couldn't sleep and I threw up the whole pregnancy. Once I peed on the stick to test for protein and it was darkest green. The next time, back to trace protein. Or plus 1. My midwives wondered about an oddity and tested the blood. Tested the urine. Trace. Plus 1. But sometimes not when I tested at home.

I called the midwives too much or, at least, more than I thought they wanted.

One midwife thought I was simply anxious. Justifiably anxious because of the first pregnancy, but still, anxious. After my second birth, she said she'd never seen a woman with preeclampsia twice. And recommended a high-risk OBGYN for subsequent pregnancies.

We didn't talk about anxiety in terms of my symptoms after the magnesium drip. Only later. And then I had the referral put through to the perinatal clinic. Postpartum anxiety. Postpartum depression. Lack of affect. Significant history of depression. CPTSD.

My other midwife was my first midwife too. She had sat with me through the long induction of my first birth, after my blood pressures rose and the baby's heart flickered. She took me seriously but still – thought I might be anxious.

Was I anxious? The odds were in its favour. Doubled preeclampsia is rare.

Lucky me.

Some photos of the birth I find difficult to see. I remember the intensity of the experience – my anxiety and the pressure building in my head. I remember what came after.

With this pregnancy, we were cautious but hopeful. Typically speaking, it's more likely in a first pregnancy. But I was unusually sick, and my instinct said something was wrong. My midwives arranged for shared care with a sympathetic but calm OBGYN. We took good care. I took baby aspirin and we waited. We hired a doula because my first birth had been so long. I painted my toenails sea green. I still hoped to birth my second baby in the water.

But.

The pressures were too high at the end. Too high for midwifery care. They still hoped to attend the birth, but it was too quick. A was born after a precipitous two-hour labour in hospital. Our doula kept me together. My birth photographer recorded the birth in photos. My husband was terrified. I hired both women because I wanted to contain my fear and put a circle around this work.

Our second daughter was caught by the nurses instead of her father as they were surprised by the quick progression. They didn't believe me when I said I was pushing. They didn't believe the doula. The midwife wasn't called. My midwife instinctively decided to check on me without being called and arrived not long after the birth.

I had to ask others what happened. My husband and I were shell-shocked. You can see it in some of the photos. Along with the relief and temporary calm.

Two nights after the birth, I felt the same squirrelly upper right quadrant pain as I had two years ago. My blurry eyesight doubled. Flashes of light. Headache growling at the corners of my brain. I waited in the dark with my two daughters for my mother to come. Another few days in hospital, more magnesium, the dark.

The doctors will be afraid of me. I scare them. Preeclampsia is unpredictable. It is also described in my records as partial HELLP—an acronym for a harsher variant impacting more systems—acronymic scream stuttering out problems with hemolysis, elevated liver enzymes, and low platelets. All are askew for me except platelets. I am a tiny percentage of a tiny percentage. But my second daughter stayed with me at hospital and the preeclampsia wasn't as severe.

The Preeclampsia Foundation notes that "preeclampsia and other hypertensive disorders of pregnancy are a leading cause of maternal and infant illness and death. By conservative estimates, these disorders are responsible for 76,000 maternal and 500,000 infant deaths each year."[6]

It impacts only 5% to 8% of pregnancies but can (rarely) run into the postpartum period. Preeclampsia is still not well understood by doctors and has been noted by the World Health Organization as an underfunded area of health research. I was fortunate to have excellent care from midwives, nurses, doctors. Unlike many other women who are not taken seriously until they are extremely ill. Unlike women in some countries without access to postpartum care.

The birth photos find the thready line before the neurological symptoms. They caught some of the joy. I can't look at them mostly. Only sometimes. I appreciate the borrowed eyes.

nesting doll

I've been told my memories are not my own.

I thought that putting shoes out for St. Nicholas was a family tradition from my mother's Eastern European family. My mother says it came from a book I read as a child, and they just went along with the ritual in addition to stockings.

My mother's family may have followed the tradition in Poland. But never here. I introduced a ghost memory to the fold.

My aunt was irritated by a story of my great-aunt after she died, that there had been a lover that no one knew about it. The story was birthed by a friend at the wake. I'm not irritated by it, and I try to parse why. I try to say—without the stories, there's barely anything left of a person. Even if the stories aren't entirely right, they breathe a bit of life into the flat images. Our memories are not our own. Your memories are not complete. Stories may not align. But she's not quite dead if she's remembered.

When I look at pictures of my daughters as babies, toddlers, preschoolers—I wonder what they'll remember of this, other than what they're told. I wonder what they'll make of themselves all bundled in the woven wraps and ring slings. If they'll understand the quiet hope and love of those things, which kept me sane in their early babydom. Now that I've had a bit more sleep, I want to reach back into the photos and bring the small ones close to me. I want to re-kind my babies. I want to rewind. I put my hand out and a small hand grasps my baby finger. I kiss the tips of their toes. I love them. I love them.

I miss the babies in the photos, and I love the wild things tumbling in front of me. I want to be a good mother. I try to be patient and kind and listen. A snapdragon of a mood rears up sometimes and I'm too sharp with my words. I try to unknot and apologize as needed.

I wonder if I die now what they'll remember of me and whether those memories will be honest. I'd want them to remember the good and the bad. I'd want them to remember that I was human, and I loved them so much and I thought they were wonderful. I'd not want to burden them with excess. Just love and strength.

Strength is relative.

I know my memory of my grandparents is contaminated by the memories of others and the stories I've heard. A sliver of something like a person though is something of a person.

I post pictures of family life on Instagram and Facebook though I know it irritates. I irritate the writers with my banality. I irritate the conservators with my poetics. I am too emotional. I am too domesticated. No part of my whole is pleasing.

I want some form of glow record for the kids. I want a touchstone for me of time and good for when I go dark.

consequence

Plein de bonnes volontés – at best we make do as we wander up hillsides shuck red pull my ditches. (I suppose I was a something somewhere I suppose I press my lips to cardamom I suppose I love disparate/ridiculous.) I am entirely unopposed and ditch walking shouldering a collapsible sink of crocodile tears – my intent less latent than descent. A fall space between knuckles I just mean to say that I suppose we are *something*.

Red-lipped, I stole a peach once and stood there eating it.

I remember qualities of hollow in a tree and how I fed it leaves. I remember my particular forms of concrete and mass. I remember those treatments to reduce inflammation. I remember a year spent grass-bed with grubs underneath. I remember the horse stirrup flanks that put hooves on paths.

What I mean is – what I said was that I know I meant it (at the time). When pen lifts where feet drop dust to ash and peach to peach. Perverse results aside: *I am not sorry.*

Butterflies batter down the hatches and keep time. I bite my fingers for the salt I walk my road I– My intent was *never.*

Endnotes

1   Portions of *Passio of St. Margaret* held by the British Library
    (BL MS Egerton 877, approx. c. 1490). See Acknowledgements
    for more information.

2   Irvine Loudon, *Death in Childbirth: An International Study of
    Maternal Care and Maternal Mortality* (1800–1950), Oxford:
    Clarendon Press, 1992.

3   Mandy J. Bell, "A Historical Overview of Preeclampsia-Eclampsia,"
    J Obstet Gynecol Neonatal Nurs. 2010 Sept.; 39(5): 510–18.

4   Mandy J. Bell, "A Historical Overview of Preeclampsia-Eclampsia,"
    J Obstet Gynecol Neonatal Nurs. 2010 Sept.; 39(5): 510–18.

5   Irvine Loudon, *Death in Childbirth: An International Study of
    Maternal Care and Maternal Mortality (1800–1950)*, Oxford:
    Clarendon Press, 1992.

6   www.medscinet.com/preeclampsia/page.aspx?id=4

List of Figures

Cover image: Collage by Kate Sutherland. Flora within image is *Cyclamen europaeum L.* Europäisches Alpenveilchen. Cyclamen roots were historically used as a purgative and for disorders of the uterus though they are incredibly toxic.

Page 10: Illumination from Eggerton 877, from the British Library archive (in public domain). This manuscript was used as a birthing aid for women during labour. The smear across the parchment is from women kissing the page invoking St. Margaret to protect them and their children in labour.

Page 23: Retinal scan of C. McNair. Due to medications, these must be done every year.

Page 32: Photo of hospital lights in a Niagara hospital by C. McNair.

Page 38: Photo of copper ring where once there was a lightning rod. Photo by C. McNair.

Page 52: *Salvitae*. Salvitae : toxemias of pregnancy / American Apothecaries Company (1920–29?). Source: Wellcome Collection, Creative Commons. CC BY 4.0 via Wikimedia Commons.

Page 59: Photo of mirrored hospital hallway by C. McNair.

Page 68: Page from Ezra Michener's *Hand-Book of Eclampsia, or, Notes and Cases of Puerperal Convulsions* (1883). Photo by C. McNair.

Pages 80–81: Munitions Production (1914–18). Young female munition workers (canary girls) filling shells in a factory at an undisclosed location. © Crown Copyright: IWM.

Page 91: Hands in lap of Irene (Irina) Lydia (Lidija) Verworn (Ferworn), age fifteen, grandmother to C. McNair. Photographer unknown.

Page 104: Photo of baby clothes owned by Rose and Aoife McLennan taken by C. McNair.

Page 113: Photo of garlic from C. McNair's garden with wild lawn taken by C. McNair.

Page 122: The shrine of Mount Carmel near Humboldt, Saskatchewan. Photo by C. McNair.

Page 130: Page from *Preeclamptic and Eclamptic Toxemia of Pregnancy* by Lewis Dexter, Florence W. Haynes, and Soma Weiss. Boston: Little and Brown, 1941. Photo by C. McNair.

Page 136: Page from Ezra Michener's *Hand-Book of Eclampsia, or, Notes and Cases of Puerperal Convulsions* (1883). Photo by C. McNair.

Page 140: Photo of blood-draw tools at Ottawa Civic Hospital. Photo by C. McNair.

Page 151: "Veratrum album L. Melanthiaceae Distribution: Europe. Cows do not eat Veratrum species in the meadows, and human poisoning with it caused vomiting and fainting. In the 1850s it was found to reduce the heart's action and slow the pulse (Bentley, 1861, called it an 'arterial sedative'), and in 1859 it was used orally in a woman who was having convulsions due to eclampsia. Dr Paul DeLacy Baker in Alabama treated her with drops of a tincture of V. viride. She recovered. It was used thereafter, as the first choice of treatment, and when blood pressure monitoring became possible, it was discovered that it worked by reducing the high blood pressure that occurs in eclampsia. By 1947 death rates were reduced from 30% to 5% by its use at the Boston Lying in Hospital. It works by dilating the arteries in muscles and in the gastrointestinal circulation. A further use of Veratrum species came to light when it was noted that V. californicum – and other species – if eaten by sheep resulted in foetal malformations, in particular only having one eye. The chemical in the plant that was responsible, cyclopamine, was found to act on certain genetic pathways responsible for stem cell division in the regulation of the development of bilateral symmetry in the embryo/foetus. Synthetic analogues have been developed which act on what have come to be called the 'hedgehog signalling pathways' in stem cell division, and these 'Hedgehog inhibitors' are being introduced into medicine for the treatment of various cancers like chondrosarcoma, myelofibrosis, and advanced basal cell carcinoma. The drugs are saridegib, erismodegib and vismodegib. All the early herbals report on its ability to cause vomiting. As a herbal medicine it is Prescription Only, via a registered dentist or physician (UK Medicines and Healthcare Products Regulatory Agency (MHRA)). Photographed in the Medicinal Garden of the

Royal College of Physicians, London. Dr Henry Oakeley." Attribution 4.0 International (CC BY 4.0). Source: Wellcome Collection.

Page 161: A delicious peach provided during peach season at a hospital in Niagara. Photo by C. McNair.

Page 172: Engraving from *The compleat midwife's practice enlarged ... With instructions of the Queen of France's midwife* by unknown (anonymous initials), fourth edition enlarged (London: 1680), p106. Photo by C. McNair.

Glossary of Terms

clot: A semi-solid mass, also known as a thrombus. A form of craft my insides love to make.

dread: A feeling of apprehension and a symptom of preeclampsia. A sense of doom.

eclampsia: When the body begins to seize after preeclampsia. See: Lady Sybil of *Downton Abbey*.

edema: Swelling. Chipmunk face and marshmallow feet.

fascinoma: An interesting medical puzzle that would make a good paper. Me.

inherent vice: A flaw at the core of a material.

HELLP syndrome: A life-threatening disorder of pregnancy that is often described as a severe form of preeclampsia with elevated liver enzymes and low platelets.

horsetail: A living fossil plant that is high in silica that reproduces by rhizomes and spores. It is said to lower blood pressure and grows in my garden uncontrollably.

hypertension: Elevated blood pressure.

magnesium sulphide: A medicine used to treat preeclampsia. It gave me a headache and made me feel untethered.

maternal morbidity: Suffering during pregnancy or just after pregnancy.

nonbacterial (or marantic) endocarditis: An extremely rare heart condition, typically associated with metastasized cancer or lupus. A craft my heart decided to make.

normalization of deviance: Occurs when it becomes generally acceptable to deviate from safety systems, procedures, and processes.

preeclampsia: A hypertensive disorder of pregnancy where the blood pressure of a pregnant person is elevated and there is protein in their urine. It is life-threatening, and those who have had preeclampsia are 7× more likely to suffer a stroke or have heart conditions later in life. Preeclampsia is the leading cause of maternal mortality, in part due to the risks of postpartum preeclampsia. Preeclampsia is a risk up to six weeks post-birth. Don't believe anyone who says delivery is the cure for preeclampsia. Incomplete answer. Minus 100 points.

thrombophilia: Clot-loving.

TIA: Transient ischemic attack or mini-stroke. A stroke where the damage doesn't stick too much, if at all. Precursor to actual stroke.

toxemia (or toxaemia) of pregnancy: The old words used to describe preeclampsia when it was believed to be poison in the blood.

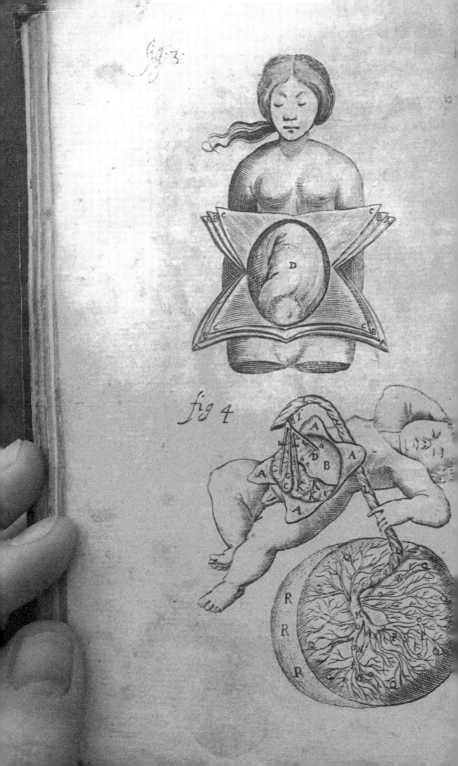

Acknowledgements

With love forever to Rob, Rose, and Aoife. Gratitude to those who offered feedback and gentle support in the early days. Namely Rob, Sandy, and Amanda. Thank you to my family both large and small.

Thank you to everyone at Book*hug Press. Thank you especially to Jay and Hazel and to my editor Tanis MacDonald for believing in this work. Tanis made this work better and her approach was exactly what this book needed.

Tanis first offered support and possibilities in the development of this manuscript at the Sage Hill Writing retreat in 2019 in her non-fiction workshop. Gratitude to my co-participants: Rayanne, Carla, Concetta, and Laurie. Gratitude to Sage Hill for having me there and to Tara for taking me out to the moon. Thank you to Nasser Hussain, who helped me work on this manuscript during the 2023 winter residency at the Banff Centre for the Arts, and to all my co-participants in the mountains.

Thank you to my midwives Maxine, Marika, Suzanne, Arlaine, Kelly, and Laurence, and the student midwives who assisted. Thanks to Dr. McCoubrey and the team of OBGYNs at the Montfort Hospital. Thanks to Elle and Pia. Thank you to the postpartum mental health treatment program at the Montfort Hospital. Thanks to my coach Debbie from the CardioPrevent postpartum program at the University of Ottawa Heart Institute.

Thank you to many doctors, nurses, therapists, and specialists who cared for me in the Terrible Year of 2019 at the Ottawa Civic Hospital, the University of Ottawa Heart Institute, the Ottawa General Hospital, and the Niagara Hospital. Thank you to my parents who made that awful year manageable, despite everything.

The partial textual charm at the beginning of the book is from an illuminated manuscript of the *Passio of St. Margaret* held by the British Library (BL MS Egerton 877, approx. c. 1490). The illuminations in this manuscript have been damaged by kissing, as it was used as a birthing aid.

The text of the poems "jamais vu" and "déjà vu" were transcribed from episode 5 of the third season of *Downton Abbey*. The text of "foliate" is a modification of information from the 1916 guide *The Mother and Her Child* by Lena K. Sadler and William S. Sadler.

Portions of this manuscript were previously published in *Canthius, Parentheses,* and *ottawater.* "Zlata baba" was previously published in the chapbook *Hexe* (shrieking violet press, 2023). With thanks to the Canada Council for the Arts, the Ontario Arts Council Research and Creation program, the Ontario Arts Council Recommenders program, and the City of Ottawa for their support in the creation of this manuscript.

About the Author

Christine McNair is the author of *Charm* (winner of the 2018 Archibald Lampman Award) and *Conflict* (finalist for the City of Ottawa Book Award, the Archibald Lampman Award, and the ReLit Award for Poetry). She was also nominated for the Robert Kroetsch Award for Innovative Poetry. Her chapbook *pleasantries and other misdemeanours* was shortlisted for the bpNichol Chapbook Award. Her work has appeared in sundry literary journals and anthologies. McNair lives in Ottawa, where she works as a book doctor.

Colophon

Manufactured as the first edition of
Toxemia
in the fall of 2024 by Book*hug Press

Edited for the press by Tanis MacDonald
Copy-edited by Stuart Ross
Proofread by Laurie Siblock
Design and typesetting by Gareth Lind, Lind Design
Cover image by Kate Sutherland. Used with permission.
Typeset in FF Good, designed by Łukasz Dziedzic

Printed in Canada

bookhugpress.ca